THE
PRAYER
MAP®
FOR
DADS

BARBOUR
PUBLISHING

Scripture taken from the HOLY BIBLE, NEW INTERNATIONAL VERSION®. NIV®. Copyright © 1973, 1978, 1984, 2011 by Biblica, Inc.™ Used by permission. All rights reserved worldwide.

Published by Barbour Publishing, Inc., 1810 Barbour Drive, Uhrichsville, Ohio 44683, www.barbourbooks.com

Our mission is to inspire the world with the life-changing message of the Bible.

Member of the
Evangelical Christian
Publishers Association

Printed in China.

WHAT DOES PRAYER LOOK LIKE? . . .

Get ready to more fully experience the power of prayer in your everyday life with this creative journal. . .where every colorful page will guide you to create your very own prayer map—as you write out specific thoughts, ideas, and lists —that you can follow (from start to finish!) as you talk to God. (Be sure to record the date on each one of your prayer maps so you can look back over time and see how God has continued to work in your life!)

The Prayer Map for Dads will not only encourage you to spend time talking with God about the things that matter most to you as a father. . . it will also help you build a healthy spiritual habit of continual prayer for life!

DEAR HEAVENLY FATHER,

THANK YOU FOR. . .

MY PRAYER FOR MY KID(S) TODAY. . .

CONCERNS I NEED TO SHARE WITH YOU. . .

I NEED YOUR PROVISION. . .

I NEED YOUR STRENGTH. . .

PLEASE GIVE ME WISDOM. . .

AMEN.

Thank You, Father,
for hearing my prayers.

"Have I not commanded you?
Be strong and courageous. Do not be afraid;
do not be discouraged, for the LORD your
God will be with you wherever you go."

JOSHUA 1:9

DATE:

DEAR HEAVENLY FATHER,

THANK YOU FOR. . .

MY PRAYER FOR MY KID(S) TODAY. . .

CONCERNS I NEED TO SHARE WITH YOU. . .

I NEED YOUR PROVISION. . .

I NEED YOUR STRENGTH. . .

$

PLEASE GIVE ME WISDOM. . .

AMEN.
Thank You, Father,
for hearing my prayers.

*These commandments. . .are to be on your hearts.
Impress them on your children. . . . Tie them as
symbols on your hands and bind them on your
foreheads. Write them on the doorframes
of your houses and on your gates.*
DEUTERONOMY 6:6–9

DATE:

DEAR HEAVENLY FATHER,

THANK YOU FOR. . .

MY PRAYER FOR MY KID(S) TODAY. . .

CONCERNS I NEED TO SHARE WITH YOU. . .

I NEED YOUR PROVISION. . .

I NEED YOUR STRENGTH. . .

PLEASE GIVE ME WISDOM. . .

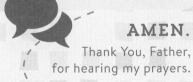

AMEN.
Thank You, Father,
for hearing my prayers.

*As a father has compassion on his children, so
the Lord has compassion on those who fear him.*
PSALM 103:13

DATE:

DEAR HEAVENLY FATHER,

....
....
....
....

THANK YOU FOR. . .

....
....
....
....
....
....

MY PRAYER FOR MY KID(S) TODAY. . .

....
....
....
....
....
....
....
....

CONCERNS I NEED TO SHARE WITH YOU. . .

....
....
....
....
....

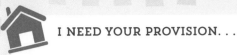

I NEED YOUR PROVISION. . .

I NEED YOUR STRENGTH. . .

PLEASE GIVE ME WISDOM. . .

AMEN.
Thank You, Father,
for hearing my prayers.

*"Choose for yourselves this day whom
you will serve. . . . But as for me and my
household, we will serve the Lord."*
JOSHUA 24:15

DATE:

DEAR HEAVENLY FATHER,

THANK YOU FOR. . .

MY PRAYER FOR MY
KID(S) TODAY. . .

CONCERNS I NEED TO SHARE WITH YOU. . .

I NEED YOUR PROVISION. . .

I NEED YOUR STRENGTH. . .

$

PLEASE GIVE ME WISDOM. . .

AMEN.
Thank You, Father,
for hearing my prayers.

My son, do not despise the Lord's discipline,
and do not resent his rebuke, because the
Lord disciplines those he loves, as a
father the son he delights in.
PROVERBS 3:11–12

DATE:

DEAR HEAVENLY FATHER,

THANK YOU FOR. . .

MY PRAYER FOR MY KID(S) TODAY. . .

CONCERNS I NEED TO SHARE WITH YOU. . .

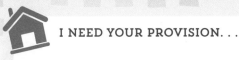

I NEED YOUR PROVISION. . .

I NEED YOUR STRENGTH. . .

PLEASE GIVE ME WISDOM. . .

AMEN.

Thank You, Father,
for hearing my prayers.

*"The LORD your God carried you,
as a father carries his son."*

DEUTERONOMY 1:31

DATE:

DEAR HEAVENLY FATHER,

THANK YOU FOR. . .

MY PRAYER FOR MY KID(S) TODAY. . .

CONCERNS I NEED TO SHARE WITH YOU. . .

I NEED YOUR PROVISION. . .

I NEED YOUR STRENGTH. . .

PLEASE GIVE ME WISDOM. . .

AMEN.
Thank You, Father,
for hearing my prayers.

Whoever fears the Lord has a secure fortress,
and for their children it will be a refuge.
PROVERBS 14:26

DATE:

DEAR HEAVENLY FATHER,

THANK YOU FOR. . .

MY PRAYER FOR MY
KID(S) TODAY. . .

CONCERNS I NEED TO SHARE WITH YOU. . .

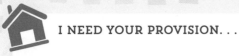 **I NEED YOUR PROVISION. . .**

....

....

....

....

I NEED YOUR STRENGTH. . .

....

....

....

....

....

....

....

....

....

....

....

PLEASE GIVE ME WISDOM. . .

....

....

....

....

....

....

....

AMEN.

Thank You, Father,
for hearing my prayers.

Children are a heritage from the LORD,
offspring a reward from him. Like arrows in the
hands of a warrior are children born in one's youth.

PSALM 127:3–4

DATE:

DEAR HEAVENLY FATHER,

THANK YOU FOR. . .

MY PRAYER FOR MY KID(S) TODAY. . .

CONCERNS I NEED TO SHARE WITH YOU. . .

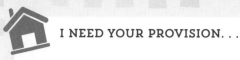

I NEED YOUR PROVISION. . .

I NEED YOUR STRENGTH. . .

PLEASE GIVE ME WISDOM. . .

AMEN.
Thank You, Father,
for hearing my prayers.

*When I was a child, I talked like a child, I thought like
a child, I reasoned like a child. When I became a man,
I put the ways of childhood behind me.*
1 CORINTHIANS 13:11

DATE:

DEAR HEAVENLY FATHER,

THANK YOU FOR. . .

MY PRAYER FOR MY KID(S) TODAY. . .

CONCERNS I NEED TO SHARE WITH YOU. . .

I NEED YOUR PROVISION. . .

I NEED YOUR STRENGTH. . .

PLEASE GIVE ME WISDOM. . .

AMEN.
Thank You, Father,
for hearing my prayers.

*"Honor your father and mother"—which is the first
commandment with a promise—"so that it may go well
with you and that you may enjoy long life on the earth."*
EPHESIANS 6:2–3

DATE:

DEAR HEAVENLY FATHER,

_____

_____

_____

_____

MY PRAYER FOR MY KID(S) TODAY. . .

_____

_____

_____

_____

_____

_____

_____

_____

THANK YOU FOR. . .

_____

_____

_____

_____

_____

_____

_____

CONCERNS I NEED TO SHARE WITH YOU. . .

_____

_____

_____

_____

I NEED YOUR PROVISION. . .

I NEED YOUR STRENGTH. . .

PLEASE GIVE ME WISDOM. . .

AMEN.

Thank You, Father,
for hearing my prayers.

*Fathers, do not exasperate your children;
instead, bring them up in the training
and instruction of the Lord.*

EPHESIANS 6:4

DATE:

DEAR HEAVENLY FATHER,

THANK YOU FOR. . .

MY PRAYER FOR MY KID(S) TODAY. . .

CONCERNS I NEED TO SHARE WITH YOU. . .

I NEED YOUR PROVISION. . .

....

....

....

....

I NEED YOUR STRENGTH. . .

....

....

....

....

....

....

....

....

....

....

....

PLEASE GIVE ME WISDOM. . .

....

....

....

....

....

....

AMEN.
Thank You, Father, for hearing my prayers.

Be on your guard; stand firm in the faith; be courageous; be strong.
1 CORINTHIANS 16:13

DATE:

DEAR HEAVENLY FATHER,

THANK YOU FOR. . .

MY PRAYER FOR MY KID(S) TODAY. . .

CONCERNS I NEED TO SHARE WITH YOU. . .

I NEED YOUR PROVISION. . .

I NEED YOUR STRENGTH. . .

PLEASE GIVE ME WISDOM. . .

AMEN.
Thank You, Father,
for hearing my prayers.

*Fathers, do not embitter your children,
or they will become discouraged.*
Colossians 3:21

DATE:

DEAR HEAVENLY FATHER,

THANK YOU FOR. . .

MY PRAYER FOR MY KID(S) TODAY. . .

CONCERNS I NEED TO SHARE WITH YOU. . .

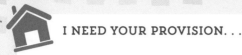

I NEED YOUR PROVISION. . .

....

....

....

....

I NEED YOUR STRENGTH. . .

....

....

....

....

....

....

....

....

....

....

PLEASE GIVE ME WISDOM. . .

....

....

....

....

....

....

AMEN.

Thank You, Father,
for hearing my prayers.

*All Scripture is God-breathed and is useful for
teaching, rebuking, correcting and training in
righteousness, so that the servant of God may
be thoroughly equipped for every good work.*

2 TIMOTHY 3:16–17

DATE:

DEAR HEAVENLY FATHER,

THANK YOU FOR. . .

MY PRAYER FOR MY KID(S) TODAY. . .

CONCERNS I NEED TO SHARE WITH YOU. . .

I NEED YOUR PROVISION. . .

I NEED YOUR STRENGTH. . .

PLEASE GIVE ME WISDOM. . .

AMEN.
Thank You, Father,
for hearing my prayers.

*"My command is this: Love each
other as I have loved you."*
JOHN 15:12

DATE:

DEAR HEAVENLY FATHER,

THANK YOU FOR. . .

MY PRAYER FOR MY KID(S) TODAY. . .

CONCERNS I NEED TO SHARE WITH YOU. . .

I NEED YOUR PROVISION. . .

....

....

....

....

I NEED YOUR STRENGTH. . .

....

....

....

....

....

....

....

....

....

....

PLEASE GIVE ME WISDOM. . .

....

....

....

....

....

....

AMEN.
Thank You, Father,
for hearing my prayers.

*The father of a righteous child has great joy;
a man who fathers a wise son rejoices in him.*
PROVERBS 23:24

DATE:

DEAR HEAVENLY FATHER,

THANK YOU FOR. . .

MY PRAYER FOR MY
KID(S) TODAY. . .

CONCERNS I NEED TO SHARE WITH YOU. . .

I NEED YOUR PROVISION. . .

I NEED YOUR STRENGTH. . .

PLEASE GIVE ME WISDOM. . .

AMEN.
Thank You, Father,
for hearing my prayers.

*My son, pay attention to what I say; turn your ear
to my words. Do not let them out of your sight,
keep them within your heart; for they are life to
those who find them and health to one's whole body.*
PROVERBS 4:20–22

DATE:

DEAR HEAVENLY FATHER,

THANK YOU FOR. . .

MY PRAYER FOR MY KID(S) TODAY. . .

CONCERNS I NEED TO SHARE WITH YOU. . .

 I NEED YOUR PROVISION. . .

I NEED YOUR STRENGTH. . .

PLEASE GIVE ME WISDOM. . .

AMEN.
Thank You, Father,
for hearing my prayers.

Whoever walks in integrity walks securely,
but whoever takes crooked paths will be found out.
PROVERBS 10:9

DATE:

DEAR HEAVENLY FATHER,

THANK YOU FOR. . .

MY PRAYER FOR MY
KID(S) TODAY. . .

CONCERNS I NEED TO SHARE WITH YOU. . .

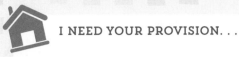

I NEED YOUR PROVISION. . .

I NEED YOUR STRENGTH. . .

PLEASE GIVE ME WISDOM. . .

AMEN.
Thank You, Father,
for hearing my prayers.

The one who has knowledge uses words with restraint,
and whoever has understanding is even-tempered.
PROVERBS 17:27

DATE:

DEAR HEAVENLY FATHER,

THANK YOU FOR. . .

MY PRAYER FOR MY KID(S) TODAY. . .

CONCERNS I NEED TO SHARE WITH YOU. . .

 I NEED YOUR PROVISION. . .

I NEED YOUR STRENGTH. . .

PLEASE GIVE ME WISDOM. . .

AMEN.
Thank You, Father,
for hearing my prayers.

Listen to your father, who gave you life, and do
not despise your mother when she is old.
PROVERBS 23:22

DATE:

DEAR HEAVENLY FATHER,

THANK YOU FOR. . .

MY PRAYER FOR MY
KID(S) TODAY. . .

CONCERNS I NEED TO SHARE WITH YOU. . .

I NEED YOUR PROVISION. . .

I NEED YOUR STRENGTH. . .

PLEASE GIVE ME WISDOM. . .

AMEN.

Thank You, Father,
for hearing my prayers.

*"Honor your father and your mother,
so that you may live long in the land
the LORD your God is giving you."*

EXODUS 20:12

DATE:

DEAR HEAVENLY FATHER,

....

....

....

....

THANK YOU FOR. . .

....

....

....

....

....

....

....

MY PRAYER FOR MY
KID(S) TODAY. . .

....

....

....

....

....

....

....

....

CONCERNS I NEED TO SHARE WITH YOU. . .

....

....

....

....

....

I NEED YOUR PROVISION. . .

I NEED YOUR STRENGTH. . .

PLEASE GIVE ME WISDOM. . .

AMEN.
Thank You, Father,
for hearing my prayers.

*Listen, my son, to your father's instruction
and do not forsake your mother's teaching.*
PROVERBS 1:8

DATE:

DEAR HEAVENLY FATHER,

THANK YOU FOR...

MY PRAYER FOR MY KID(S) TODAY...

CONCERNS I NEED TO SHARE WITH YOU...

I NEED YOUR PROVISION. . .

I NEED YOUR STRENGTH. . .

PLEASE GIVE ME WISDOM. . .

AMEN.
Thank You, Father,
for hearing my prayers.

*A good person leaves an inheritance for
their children's children, but a sinner's
wealth is stored up for the righteous.*
PROVERBS 13:22

DATE:

DEAR HEAVENLY FATHER,

THANK YOU FOR. . .

MY PRAYER FOR MY KID(S) TODAY. . .

CONCERNS I NEED TO SHARE WITH YOU. . .

I NEED YOUR PROVISION. . .

I NEED YOUR STRENGTH. . .

PLEASE GIVE ME WISDOM. . .

AMEN.
Thank You, Father,
for hearing my prayers.

*I have no greater joy than to hear that
my children are walking in the truth.*
3 JOHN 1:4

DATE:

DEAR HEAVENLY FATHER,

THANK YOU FOR. . .

MY PRAYER FOR MY KID(S) TODAY. . .

CONCERNS I NEED TO SHARE WITH YOU. . .

I NEED YOUR PROVISION. . .

I NEED YOUR STRENGTH. . .

PLEASE GIVE ME WISDOM. . .

AMEN.
Thank You, Father,
for hearing my prayers.

*Start children off on the way they should go,
and even when they are old they will not turn from it.*
PROVERBS 22:6

DATE:

DEAR HEAVENLY FATHER,

THANK YOU FOR. . .

MY PRAYER FOR MY KID(S) TODAY. . .

CONCERNS I NEED TO SHARE WITH YOU. . .

I NEED YOUR PROVISION. . .

I NEED YOUR STRENGTH. . .

PLEASE GIVE ME WISDOM. . .

AMEN.
Thank You, Father,
for hearing my prayers.

May your father and mother rejoice;
may she who gave you birth be joyful!
PROVERBS 23:25

DATE:

DEAR HEAVENLY FATHER,

....

....

....

....

MY PRAYER FOR MY
KID(S) TODAY. . .

....

....

....

....

....

....

THANK YOU FOR. . .

....

....

....

....

....

....

CONCERNS I NEED TO SHARE WITH YOU. . .

....

....

....

....

I NEED YOUR PROVISION. . .

I NEED YOUR STRENGTH. . .

PLEASE GIVE ME WISDOM. . .

AMEN.
Thank You, Father,
for hearing my prayers.

*"Believe in the Lord Jesus, and you will
be saved—you and your household."*
ACTS 16:31

DATE:

DEAR HEAVENLY FATHER,

....
....
....
....

THANK YOU FOR. . .

....
....
....
....
....
....
....

MY PRAYER FOR MY KID(S) TODAY. . .

....
....
....
....
....
....
....
....

CONCERNS I NEED TO SHARE WITH YOU. . .

....
....
....
....

I NEED YOUR PROVISION. . .

I NEED YOUR STRENGTH. . .

PLEASE GIVE ME WISDOM. . .

AMEN.

Thank You, Father,
for hearing my prayers.

*How good and pleasant it is when
God's people live together in unity!*

PSALM 133:1

DATE:

DEAR HEAVENLY FATHER,

THANK YOU FOR. . .

MY PRAYER FOR MY
KID(S) TODAY. . .

CONCERNS I NEED TO SHARE WITH YOU. . .

I NEED YOUR PROVISION. . .

I NEED YOUR STRENGTH. . .

PLEASE GIVE ME WISDOM. . .

AMEN.
Thank You, Father,
for hearing my prayers.

The righteous lead blameless lives;
blessed are their children after them.
PROVERBS 20:7

DATE:

DEAR HEAVENLY FATHER,

THANK YOU FOR. . .

MY PRAYER FOR MY
KID(S) TODAY. . .

CONCERNS I NEED TO SHARE WITH YOU. . .

I NEED YOUR PROVISION. . .

I NEED YOUR
STRENGTH. . .

PLEASE GIVE ME WISDOM. . .

AMEN.
Thank You, Father,
for hearing my prayers.

Yet you, LORD, are our Father. We are the clay,
you are the potter; we are all the work of your hand.
ISAIAH 64:8

DATE:

DEAR HEAVENLY FATHER,

THANK YOU FOR. . .

MY PRAYER FOR MY
KID(S) TODAY. . .

CONCERNS I NEED TO SHARE WITH YOU. . .

I NEED YOUR PROVISION. . .

I NEED YOUR STRENGTH. . .

PLEASE GIVE ME WISDOM. . .

AMEN.
Thank You, Father,
for hearing my prayers.

"Assemble the people before me to hear my words so
that they may learn to revere me as long as they live
in the land and may teach them to their children."

DEUTERONOMY 4:10

DATE:

DEAR HEAVENLY FATHER,

THANK YOU FOR. . .

MY PRAYER FOR MY KID(S) TODAY. . .

CONCERNS I NEED TO SHARE WITH YOU. . .

I NEED YOUR PROVISION. . .

I NEED YOUR STRENGTH. . .

PLEASE GIVE ME WISDOM. . .

AMEN.
Thank You, Father,
for hearing my prayers.

"Therefore go and make disciples of all nations,
baptizing them in the name of the Father
and of the Son and of the Holy Spirit."
MATTHEW 28:19

DATE:

DEAR HEAVENLY FATHER,

THANK YOU FOR. . .

MY PRAYER FOR MY KID(S) TODAY. . .

CONCERNS I NEED TO SHARE WITH YOU. . .

I NEED YOUR PROVISION. . .

I NEED YOUR STRENGTH. . .

PLEASE GIVE ME WISDOM. . .

AMEN.
Thank You, Father,
for hearing my prayers.

Above all, love each other deeply,
because love covers over a multitude of sins.
1 PETER 4:8

DATE:

DEAR HEAVENLY FATHER,

THANK YOU FOR. . .

MY PRAYER FOR MY
KID(S) TODAY. . .

CONCERNS I NEED TO SHARE WITH YOU. . .

I NEED YOUR PROVISION. . .

I NEED YOUR STRENGTH. . .

PLEASE GIVE ME WISDOM. . .

AMEN.
Thank You, Father,
for hearing my prayers.

*Be joyful in hope, patient in
affliction, faithful in prayer.*
ROMANS 12:12

DATE:

DEAR HEAVENLY FATHER,

....
....
....
....

MY PRAYER FOR MY
KID(S) TODAY. . .

....

THANK YOU FOR. . .

....
....
....
....
....
....
....

CONCERNS I NEED TO SHARE WITH YOU. . .

....
....
....
....

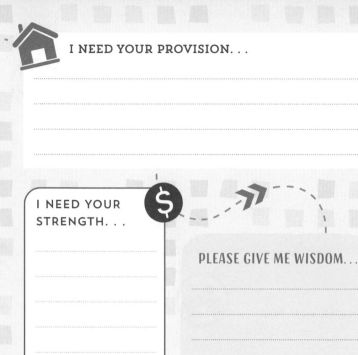

I NEED YOUR PROVISION. . .

I NEED YOUR STRENGTH. . .

PLEASE GIVE ME WISDOM. . .

AMEN.
Thank You, Father,
for hearing my prayers.

*Endure hardship as discipline; God is treating
you as his children. For what children are
not disciplined by their father?*
HEBREWS 12:7

DATE:

DEAR HEAVENLY FATHER,

....
....
....
....

THANK YOU FOR. . .

....
....
....
....
....
....

MY PRAYER FOR MY KID(S) TODAY. . .

....
....
....
....
....
....
....

CONCERNS I NEED TO SHARE WITH YOU. . .

....
....
....
....

I NEED YOUR PROVISION. . .

....

....

....

....

I NEED YOUR STRENGTH. . .

....

....

....

....

....

....

....

....

....

....

....

PLEASE GIVE ME WISDOM. . .

....

....

....

....

....

....

....

AMEN.
Thank You, Father,
for hearing my prayers.

*For the Spirit God gave us does not make us timid,
but gives us power, love and self-discipline.*
2 TIMOTHY 1:7

DATE:

DEAR HEAVENLY FATHER,

....

....

....

....

THANK YOU FOR. . .

....

....

....

....

....

....

....

MY PRAYER FOR MY
KID(S) TODAY. . .

....

....

....

....

....

....

....

....

CONCERNS I NEED TO SHARE WITH YOU. . .

....

....

....

....

I NEED YOUR PROVISION. . .

I NEED YOUR STRENGTH. . .

PLEASE GIVE ME WISDOM. . .

AMEN.
Thank You, Father,
for hearing my prayers.

*"For I have chosen him, so that he will direct his
children and his household after him to keep the
way of the LORD by doing what is right and just."*
GENESIS 18:19

DATE:

DEAR HEAVENLY FATHER,

THANK YOU FOR. . .

MY PRAYER FOR MY
KID(S) TODAY. . .

CONCERNS I NEED TO SHARE WITH YOU. . .

I NEED YOUR PROVISION. . .

....

....

....

....

I NEED YOUR STRENGTH. . .

....

....

....

....

....

....

....

....

....

....

PLEASE GIVE ME WISDOM. . .

....

....

....

....

....

....

AMEN.
Thank You, Father,
for hearing my prayers.

*And God is able to bless you abundantly, so that
in all things at all times, having all that you need,
you will abound in every good work.*
2 CORINTHIANS 9:8

DATE:

DEAR HEAVENLY FATHER,

MY PRAYER FOR MY
KID(S) TODAY. . .

THANK YOU FOR. . .

CONCERNS I NEED TO SHARE WITH YOU. . .

I NEED YOUR PROVISION. . .

I NEED YOUR STRENGTH. . .

PLEASE GIVE ME WISDOM. . .

AMEN.
Thank You, Father,
for hearing my prayers.

*Put on the full armor of God, so that you can
take your stand against the devil's schemes.*
EPHESIANS 6:11

DATE:

DEAR HEAVENLY FATHER,

THANK YOU FOR. . .

MY PRAYER FOR MY
KID(S) TODAY. . .

CONCERNS I NEED TO SHARE WITH YOU. . .

I NEED YOUR PROVISION. . .

I NEED YOUR STRENGTH. . .

PLEASE GIVE ME WISDOM. . .

AMEN.

Thank You, Father,
for hearing my prayers.

The LORD is my strength and my shield;
my heart trusts in him, and he helps me.

PSALM 28:7

DATE:

DEAR HEAVENLY FATHER,

THANK YOU FOR. . .

MY PRAYER FOR MY KID(S) TODAY. . .

CONCERNS I NEED TO SHARE WITH YOU. . .

I NEED YOUR PROVISION. . .

I NEED YOUR STRENGTH. . .

PLEASE GIVE ME WISDOM. . .

AMEN.
Thank You, Father,
for hearing my prayers.

*For what you have done I will always praise you
in the presence of your faithful people. And I will
hope in your name, for your name is good.*
PSALM 52:9

DATE:

DEAR HEAVENLY FATHER,

THANK YOU FOR. . .

MY PRAYER FOR MY KID(S) TODAY. . .

CONCERNS I NEED TO SHARE WITH YOU. . .

I NEED YOUR PROVISION. . .

....

....

....

....

I NEED YOUR STRENGTH. . .

....

....

....

....

....

....

....

....

....

....

PLEASE GIVE ME WISDOM. . .

....

....

....

....

....

....

AMEN.

Thank You, Father, for hearing my prayers.

Asa did what was right in the eyes of the LORD, as his father David had done.

1 KINGS 15:11

DATE:

DEAR HEAVENLY FATHER,

THANK YOU FOR. . .

MY PRAYER FOR MY
KID(S) TODAY. . .

CONCERNS I NEED TO SHARE WITH YOU. . .

I NEED YOUR PROVISION. . .

....

....

....

....

I NEED YOUR STRENGTH. . .

....

....

....

....

....

....

....

....

....

....

PLEASE GIVE ME WISDOM. . .

....

....

....

....

....

....

AMEN.

Thank You, Father,
for hearing my prayers.

The LORD is good, a refuge in times of trouble.
He cares for those who trust in him.
NAHUM 1:7

DATE:

DEAR HEAVENLY FATHER,

THANK YOU FOR. . .

MY PRAYER FOR MY
KID(S) TODAY. . .

CONCERNS I NEED TO SHARE WITH YOU. . .

I NEED YOUR PROVISION. . .

I NEED YOUR STRENGTH. . .

PLEASE GIVE ME WISDOM. . .

AMEN.
Thank You, Father,
for hearing my prayers.

*"I know, my God, that you test the heart and are pleased
with integrity. All these things I have given willingly and
with honest intent. And now I have seen with joy how
willingly your people who are here have given to you."*
1 CHRONICLES 29:17

DATE:

DEAR HEAVENLY FATHER,

THANK YOU FOR. . .

MY PRAYER FOR MY KID(S) TODAY. . .

CONCERNS I NEED TO SHARE WITH YOU. . .

I NEED YOUR PROVISION. . .

I NEED YOUR STRENGTH. . .

PLEASE GIVE ME WISDOM. . .

AMEN.

Thank You, Father,
for hearing my prayers.

Listen, my sons, to a father's instruction; pay attention and gain understanding. I give you sound learning, so do not forsake my teaching. For I too was a son to my father. . . . Then he taught me, and he said to me, "Take hold of my words with all your heart; keep my commands, and you will live."

PROVERBS 4:1–4

DATE:

DEAR HEAVENLY FATHER,

THANK YOU FOR. . .

MY PRAYER FOR MY
KID(S) TODAY. . .

CONCERNS I NEED TO SHARE WITH YOU. . .

I NEED YOUR PROVISION. . .

I NEED YOUR STRENGTH. . .

PLEASE GIVE ME WISDOM. . .

AMEN.
Thank You, Father,
for hearing my prayers.

And now, dear children, continue in him, so that
when he appears we may be confident and
unashamed before him at his coming.
1 JOHN 2:28

DATE:

DEAR HEAVENLY FATHER,

THANK YOU FOR. . .

MY PRAYER FOR MY
KID(S) TODAY. . .

CONCERNS I NEED TO SHARE WITH YOU. . .

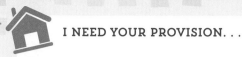

I NEED YOUR PROVISION. . .

I NEED YOUR STRENGTH. . .

PLEASE GIVE ME WISDOM. . .

AMEN.
Thank You, Father,
for hearing my prayers.

In every situation, by prayer and petition,
with thanksgiving, present your requests to God.
PHILIPPIANS 4:6

DATE:

DEAR HEAVENLY FATHER,

THANK YOU FOR. . .

MY PRAYER FOR MY KID(S) TODAY. . .

CONCERNS I NEED TO SHARE WITH YOU. . .

I NEED YOUR PROVISION. . .

....

....

....

....

I NEED YOUR STRENGTH. . .

$

....

....

....

....

....

....

....

....

....

....

PLEASE GIVE ME WISDOM. . .

....

....

....

....

....

....

AMEN.

Thank You, Father,
for hearing my prayers.

*Let the message of Christ dwell among you richly
as you teach and admonish one another with all
wisdom through psalms, hymns, and songs from the
Spirit, singing to God with gratitude in your hearts.*

COLOSSIANS 3:16

DATE:

DEAR HEAVENLY FATHER,

THANK YOU FOR. . .

MY PRAYER FOR MY
KID(S) TODAY. . .

CONCERNS I NEED TO SHARE WITH YOU. . .

 **I NEED YOUR PROVISION...**

....

....

....

....

I NEED YOUR STRENGTH...

....

....

....

....

....

....

....

....

....

PLEASE GIVE ME WISDOM...

....

....

....

....

....

....

AMEN.
Thank You, Father,
for hearing my prayers.

*"Watch and pray so that you will
not fall into temptation. The spirit
is willing, but the flesh is weak."*
MATTHEW 26:41

DATE:

DEAR HEAVENLY FATHER,

THANK YOU FOR. . .

MY PRAYER FOR MY KID(S) TODAY. . .

CONCERNS I NEED TO SHARE WITH YOU. . .

I NEED YOUR PROVISION. . .

I NEED YOUR STRENGTH. . .

PLEASE GIVE ME WISDOM. . .

AMEN.
Thank You, Father,
for hearing my prayers.

Be strong and take heart,
all you who hope in the LORD.
PSALM 31:24

DATE:

DEAR HEAVENLY FATHER,

THANK YOU FOR. . .

MY PRAYER FOR MY
KID(S) TODAY. . .

CONCERNS I NEED TO SHARE WITH YOU. . .

I NEED YOUR PROVISION. . .

I NEED YOUR STRENGTH. . .

PLEASE GIVE ME WISDOM. . .

AMEN.
Thank You, Father,
for hearing my prayers.

*"Blessed are those who listen to me, watching
daily at my doors, waiting at my doorway."*
PROVERBS 8:34

DATE:

DEAR HEAVENLY FATHER,

THANK YOU FOR. . .

MY PRAYER FOR MY KID(S) TODAY. . .

CONCERNS I NEED TO SHARE WITH YOU. . .

I NEED YOUR PROVISION. . .

I NEED YOUR STRENGTH. . .

PLEASE GIVE ME WISDOM. . .

AMEN.
Thank You, Father,
for hearing my prayers.

*So in Christ Jesus you are all
children of God through faith.*
GALATIANS 3:26

DATE:

DEAR HEAVENLY FATHER,

THANK YOU FOR. . .

MY PRAYER FOR MY KID(S) TODAY. . .

CONCERNS I NEED TO SHARE WITH YOU. . .

I NEED YOUR PROVISION. . .

I NEED YOUR STRENGTH. . .

$

PLEASE GIVE ME WISDOM. . .

AMEN.
Thank You, Father,
for hearing my prayers.

You, Lord, are forgiving and good,
abounding in love to all who call to you.
PSALM 86:5

DEAR HEAVENLY FATHER,

THANK YOU FOR. . .

MY PRAYER FOR MY KID(S) TODAY. . .

CONCERNS I NEED TO SHARE WITH YOU. . .

I NEED YOUR PROVISION. . .

I NEED YOUR STRENGTH. . .

PLEASE GIVE ME WISDOM. . .

AMEN.
Thank You, Father,
for hearing my prayers.

*Trust in the LORD with all your heart and
lean not on your own understanding.*
PROVERBS 3:5

DATE:

DEAR HEAVENLY FATHER,

THANK YOU FOR. . .

MY PRAYER FOR MY
KID(S) TODAY. . .

CONCERNS I NEED TO SHARE WITH YOU. . .

I NEED YOUR PROVISION. . .

I NEED YOUR STRENGTH. . .

PLEASE GIVE ME WISDOM. . .

AMEN.
Thank You, Father,
for hearing my prayers.

I sought the LORD, and he answered me;
he delivered me from all my fears.
PSALM 34:4

DATE:

DEAR HEAVENLY FATHER,

THANK YOU FOR. . .

MY PRAYER FOR MY KID(S) TODAY. . .

CONCERNS I NEED TO SHARE WITH YOU. . .

I NEED YOUR PROVISION. . .

I NEED YOUR STRENGTH. . .

PLEASE GIVE ME WISDOM. . .

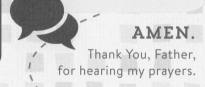

AMEN.
Thank You, Father,
for hearing my prayers.

*He tends his flock like a shepherd: He gathers the
lambs in his arms and carries them close to his
heart; he gently leads those that have young.*
ISAIAH 40:11

DATE:

DEAR HEAVENLY FATHER,

THANK YOU FOR. . .

MY PRAYER FOR MY KID(S) TODAY. . .

CONCERNS I NEED TO SHARE WITH YOU. . .

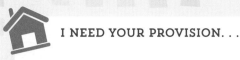

I NEED YOUR PROVISION. . .

I NEED YOUR STRENGTH. . .

PLEASE GIVE ME WISDOM. . .

AMEN.
Thank You, Father,
for hearing my prayers.

*And my God will meet all your needs according
to the riches of his glory in Christ Jesus.*
PHILIPPIANS 4:19

DATE:

DEAR HEAVENLY FATHER,

THANK YOU FOR. . .

MY PRAYER FOR MY
KID(S) TODAY. . .

CONCERNS I NEED TO SHARE WITH YOU. . .

I NEED YOUR PROVISION. . .

I NEED YOUR STRENGTH. . .

PLEASE GIVE ME WISDOM. . .

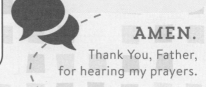

AMEN.
Thank You, Father,
for hearing my prayers.

*But you, Lord, are a compassionate
and gracious God, slow to anger,
abounding in love and faithfulness.*
PSALM 86:15

DATE:

DEAR HEAVENLY FATHER,

THANK YOU FOR. . .

MY PRAYER FOR MY KID(S) TODAY. . .

CONCERNS I NEED TO SHARE WITH YOU. . .

I NEED YOUR PROVISION. . .

....

....

....

....

I NEED YOUR STRENGTH. . .

....

....

....

....

....

....

....

....

....

....

PLEASE GIVE ME WISDOM. . .

....

....

....

....

....

....

AMEN.
Thank You, Father,
for hearing my prayers.

I cry to you, Lord; I say, "You are my refuge,
my portion in the land of the living."
Psalm 142:5

DATE:

DEAR HEAVENLY FATHER,

THANK YOU FOR. . .

MY PRAYER FOR MY KID(S) TODAY. . .

CONCERNS I NEED TO SHARE WITH YOU. . .

I NEED YOUR PROVISION. . .

I NEED YOUR STRENGTH. . .

PLEASE GIVE ME WISDOM. . .

AMEN.
Thank You, Father,
for hearing my prayers.

*Always giving thanks to God the Father for everything,
in the name of our Lord Jesus Christ.*
EPHESIANS 5:20

DATE:

DEAR HEAVENLY FATHER,

THANK YOU FOR. . .

MY PRAYER FOR MY KID(S) TODAY. . .

CONCERNS I NEED TO SHARE WITH YOU. . .

I NEED YOUR PROVISION. . .

I NEED YOUR STRENGTH. . .

PLEASE GIVE ME WISDOM. . .

AMEN.
Thank You, Father,
for hearing my prayers.

Praise be to the Lord, to God our Savior,
who daily bears our burdens.
PSALM 68:19

DATE:

DEAR HEAVENLY FATHER,

THANK YOU FOR. . .

MY PRAYER FOR MY
KID(S) TODAY. . .

CONCERNS I NEED TO SHARE WITH YOU. . .

I NEED YOUR PROVISION. . .

....

....

....

....

I NEED YOUR STRENGTH. . .

$

....

....

....

....

....

....

....

....

....

....

PLEASE GIVE ME WISDOM. . .

....

....

....

....

....

....

AMEN.
Thank You, Father,
for hearing my prayers.

The prospect of the righteous is joy.
PROVERBS 10:28

DEAR HEAVENLY FATHER,

THANK YOU FOR. . .

MY PRAYER FOR MY KID(S) TODAY. . .

CONCERNS I NEED TO SHARE WITH YOU. . .

I NEED YOUR PROVISION. . .

I NEED YOUR STRENGTH. . .

PLEASE GIVE ME WISDOM. . .

AMEN.
Thank You, Father,
for hearing my prayers.

*"But blessed is the one who trusts in
the LORD, whose confidence is in him."*
JEREMIAH 17:7

DATE: »

DEAR HEAVENLY FATHER,

....
....
....
....

THANK YOU FOR. . .

....
....
....
....
....
....
....

MY PRAYER FOR MY
KID(S) TODAY. . .

....
....
....
....
....
....
....
....
....

CONCERNS I NEED TO SHARE WITH YOU. . .

....
....
....
....

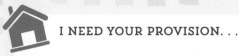

I NEED YOUR PROVISION. . .

I NEED YOUR STRENGTH. . .

PLEASE GIVE ME WISDOM. . .

AMEN.
Thank You, Father,
for hearing my prayers.

*May the God of hope fill you with all joy and peace
as you trust in him, so that you may overflow
with hope by the power of the Holy Spirit.*
ROMANS 15:13

DATE:

DEAR HEAVENLY FATHER,

THANK YOU FOR. . .

MY PRAYER FOR MY
KID(S) TODAY. . .

CONCERNS I NEED TO SHARE WITH YOU. . .

I NEED YOUR PROVISION. . .

I NEED YOUR STRENGTH. . .

PLEASE GIVE ME WISDOM. . .

AMEN.
Thank You, Father,
for hearing my prayers.

As for me, I will always have hope;
I will praise you more and more.
PSALM 71:14

DATE:

DEAR HEAVENLY FATHER,

....
....
....
....

THANK YOU FOR. . .

....
....
....
....
....
....

MY PRAYER FOR MY KID(S) TODAY. . .

....
....
....
....
....
....
....
....

CONCERNS I NEED TO SHARE WITH YOU. . .

....
....
....
....

I NEED YOUR PROVISION. . .

I NEED YOUR STRENGTH. . .

PLEASE GIVE ME WISDOM. . .

AMEN.
Thank You, Father,
for hearing my prayers.

*Let us hold unswervingly to the hope we profess,
for he who promised is faithful.*
HEBREWS 10:23

DATE:

DEAR HEAVENLY FATHER,

THANK YOU FOR. . .

MY PRAYER FOR MY
KID(S) TODAY. . .

CONCERNS I NEED TO SHARE WITH YOU. . .

I NEED YOUR PROVISION. . .

....
....
....
....

I NEED YOUR STRENGTH. . .

....
....
....
....
....
....
....
....
....
....

PLEASE GIVE ME WISDOM. . .

....
....
....
....
....
....

AMEN.

Thank You, Father,
for hearing my prayers.

*Cause me to understand the way of your precepts,
that I may meditate on your wonderful deeds.*

PSALM 119:27

DATE:

DEAR HEAVENLY FATHER,

THANK YOU FOR. . .

MY PRAYER FOR MY KID(S) TODAY. . .

CONCERNS I NEED TO SHARE WITH YOU. . .

I NEED YOUR PROVISION. . .

I NEED YOUR STRENGTH. . .

PLEASE GIVE ME WISDOM. . .

AMEN.
Thank You, Father,
for hearing my prayers.

Righteousness and justice are the foundation of your throne; love and faithfulness go before you.
PSALM 89:14

DATE:

DEAR HEAVENLY FATHER,

THANK YOU FOR. . .

MY PRAYER FOR MY KID(S) TODAY. . .

CONCERNS I NEED TO SHARE WITH YOU. . .

I NEED YOUR PROVISION. . .

I NEED YOUR STRENGTH. . .

PLEASE GIVE ME WISDOM. . .

AMEN.
Thank You, Father,
for hearing my prayers.

*Whatever you have learned or received or heard
from me, or seen in me—put it into practice.
And the God of peace will be with you.*

PHILIPPIANS 4:9

DATE:

DEAR HEAVENLY FATHER,

THANK YOU FOR. . .

MY PRAYER FOR MY KID(S) TODAY. . .

CONCERNS I NEED TO SHARE WITH YOU. . .

I NEED YOUR PROVISION. . .

I NEED YOUR STRENGTH. . .

PLEASE GIVE ME WISDOM. . .

AMEN.
Thank You, Father,
for hearing my prayers.

For you have been my hope, Sovereign LORD,
my confidence since my youth.
PSALM 71:5

DATE:

DEAR HEAVENLY FATHER,

THANK YOU FOR. . .

MY PRAYER FOR MY KID(S) TODAY. . .

CONCERNS I NEED TO SHARE WITH YOU. . .

I NEED YOUR PROVISION. . .

I NEED YOUR STRENGTH. . .

PLEASE GIVE ME WISDOM. . .

AMEN.
Thank You, Father,
for hearing my prayers.

*"Blessed rather are those who hear
the word of God and obey it."*
LUKE 11:28

DATE:

DEAR HEAVENLY FATHER,

THANK YOU FOR. . .

MY PRAYER FOR MY
KID(S) TODAY. . .

CONCERNS I NEED TO SHARE WITH YOU. . .

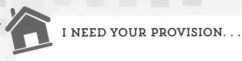

I NEED YOUR PROVISION. . .

I NEED YOUR STRENGTH. . .

PLEASE GIVE ME WISDOM. . .

AMEN.
Thank You, Father,
for hearing my prayers.

*And the Lord's servant must. . .be kind to
everyone, able to teach, not resentful.*
2 TIMOTHY 2:24

DATE:

DEAR HEAVENLY FATHER,

THANK YOU FOR. . .

MY PRAYER FOR MY KID(S) TODAY. . .

CONCERNS I NEED TO SHARE WITH YOU. . .

I NEED YOUR PROVISION. . .

I NEED YOUR STRENGTH. . .

PLEASE GIVE ME WISDOM. . .

AMEN.
Thank You, Father,
for hearing my prayers.

*Be alert and of sober mind
so that you may pray.*
1 PETER 4:7

DATE:

DEAR HEAVENLY FATHER,

MY PRAYER FOR MY
KID(S) TODAY. . .

THANK YOU FOR. . .

CONCERNS I NEED TO SHARE WITH YOU. . .

I NEED YOUR PROVISION. . .

I NEED YOUR STRENGTH. . .

PLEASE GIVE ME WISDOM. . .

AMEN.
Thank You, Father,
for hearing my prayers.

*Evildoers do not understand what is right,
but those who seek the LORD understand it fully.*
PROVERBS 28:5

DATE:

DEAR HEAVENLY FATHER,

THANK YOU FOR. . .

MY PRAYER FOR MY
KID(S) TODAY. . .

CONCERNS I NEED TO SHARE WITH YOU. . .

I NEED YOUR PROVISION. . .

I NEED YOUR STRENGTH. . .

PLEASE GIVE ME WISDOM. . .

AMEN.
Thank You, Father,
for hearing my prayers.

*You will keep in perfect peace those whose minds
are steadfast, because they trust in you.*
ISAIAH 26:3

DATE:

DEAR HEAVENLY FATHER,

....
....
....
....

THANK YOU FOR. . .

....
....
....
....
....
....

MY PRAYER FOR MY KID(S) TODAY. . .

....
....
....
....
....
....
....
....

CONCERNS I NEED TO SHARE WITH YOU. . .

....
....
....
....

I NEED YOUR PROVISION. . .

I NEED YOUR STRENGTH. . .

PLEASE GIVE ME WISDOM. . .

AMEN.
Thank You, Father,
for hearing my prayers.

Many, Lord my God, are the wonders you have done,
the things you planned for us. None can compare
with you; were I to speak and tell of your deeds,
they would be too many to declare.

PSALM 40:5

DATE:

DEAR HEAVENLY FATHER,

....

....

....

....

THANK YOU FOR. . .

....

....

....

....

....

....

MY PRAYER FOR MY KID(S) TODAY. . .

....

....

....

....

....

....

....

....

....

CONCERNS I NEED TO SHARE WITH YOU. . .

....

....

....

....

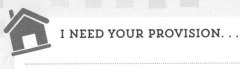

I NEED YOUR PROVISION. . .

....
....
....
....

I NEED YOUR STRENGTH. . .

....
....
....
....
....
....
....
....
....
....

PLEASE GIVE ME WISDOM. . .

....
....
....
....
....
....
....

AMEN.
Thank You, Father,
for hearing my prayers.

*As Scripture says, "Anyone who believes
in him will never be put to shame."*
ROMANS 10:11

DATE:

DEAR HEAVENLY FATHER,

THANK YOU FOR. . .

MY PRAYER FOR MY KID(S) TODAY. . .

CONCERNS I NEED TO SHARE WITH YOU. . .

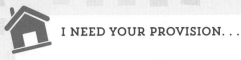

I NEED YOUR PROVISION. . .

....

....

....

....

I NEED YOUR STRENGTH. . .

....

....

....

....

....

....

....

....

....

....

PLEASE GIVE ME WISDOM. . .

....

....

....

....

....

....

AMEN.
Thank You, Father,
for hearing my prayers.

*"Peace I leave with you; my peace I give you.
I do not give to you as the world gives. Do not
let your hearts be troubled and do not be afraid."*
JOHN 14:27

DATE:

DEAR HEAVENLY FATHER,

THANK YOU FOR. . .

MY PRAYER FOR MY KID(S) TODAY. . .

CONCERNS I NEED TO SHARE WITH YOU. . .

I NEED YOUR PROVISION. . .

I NEED YOUR STRENGTH. . .

PLEASE GIVE ME WISDOM. . .

AMEN.
Thank You, Father,
for hearing my prayers.

Great peace have those who love your law,
and nothing can make them stumble.
PSALM 119:165

DATE:

DEAR HEAVENLY FATHER,

THANK YOU FOR. . .

MY PRAYER FOR MY
KID(S) TODAY. . .

CONCERNS I NEED TO SHARE WITH YOU. . .

I NEED YOUR PROVISION. . .

....

....

....

....

I NEED YOUR STRENGTH. . .

....

....

....

....

....

....

....

....

PLEASE GIVE ME WISDOM. . .

....

....

....

....

....

AMEN.
Thank You, Father,
for hearing my prayers.

*"The grass withers and the flowers fall,
but the word of our God endures forever."*
ISAIAH 40:8

DATE:

DEAR HEAVENLY FATHER,

THANK YOU FOR. . .

MY PRAYER FOR MY KID(S) TODAY. . .

CONCERNS I NEED TO SHARE WITH YOU. . .

I NEED YOUR PROVISION. . .

....

....

....

....

I NEED YOUR STRENGTH. . .

PLEASE GIVE ME WISDOM. . .

AMEN.

Thank You, Father,
for hearing my prayers.

*"The eternal God is your refuge,
and underneath are the everlasting arms."*

DEUTERONOMY 33:27

DATE:

DEAR HEAVENLY FATHER,

THANK YOU FOR. . .

MY PRAYER FOR MY KID(S) TODAY. . .

CONCERNS I NEED TO SHARE WITH YOU. . .

I NEED YOUR PROVISION. . .

I NEED YOUR STRENGTH. . .

PLEASE GIVE ME WISDOM. . .

AMEN.
Thank You, Father,
for hearing my prayers.

A hot-tempered person stirs up conflict,
but the one who is patient calms a quarrel.
PROVERBS 15:18

DATE:

DEAR HEAVENLY FATHER,

THANK YOU FOR. . .

MY PRAYER FOR MY KID(S) TODAY. . .

CONCERNS I NEED TO SHARE WITH YOU. . .

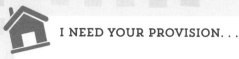

I NEED YOUR PROVISION. . .

I NEED YOUR STRENGTH. . .

PLEASE GIVE ME WISDOM. . .

AMEN.
Thank You, Father,
for hearing my prayers.

*"Ask and it will be given to you; seek and you will find;
knock and the door will be opened to you. For everyone
who asks receives; the one who seeks finds; and to the
one who knocks, the door will be opened."*

MATTHEW 7:7–8

DATE:

DEAR HEAVENLY FATHER,

....

....

....

....

MY PRAYER FOR MY KID(S) TODAY. . .

....

....

....

....

....

....

....

THANK YOU FOR. . .

....

....

....

....

....

....

....

CONCERNS I NEED TO SHARE WITH YOU. . .

....

....

....

....

I NEED YOUR PROVISION. . .

I NEED YOUR STRENGTH. . .

PLEASE GIVE ME WISDOM. . .

AMEN.
Thank You, Father,
for hearing my prayers.

Answer me when I call to you,
my righteous God.
PSALM 4:1

DATE:

DEAR HEAVENLY FATHER,

THANK YOU FOR. . .

MY PRAYER FOR MY KID(S) TODAY. . .

CONCERNS I NEED TO SHARE WITH YOU. . .

I NEED YOUR PROVISION. . .

I NEED YOUR STRENGTH. . .

PLEASE GIVE ME WISDOM. . .

AMEN.
Thank You, Father,
for hearing my prayers.

Like newborn babies, crave pure spiritual milk,
so that by it you may grow up in your salvation,
now that you have tasted that the Lord is good.
1 PETER 2:2–3

DATE:

DEAR HEAVENLY FATHER,

THANK YOU FOR. . .

MY PRAYER FOR MY KID(S) TODAY. . .

CONCERNS I NEED TO SHARE WITH YOU. . .

I NEED YOUR PROVISION. . .

I NEED YOUR STRENGTH. . .

PLEASE GIVE ME WISDOM. . .

AMEN.
Thank You, Father,
for hearing my prayers.

Pray continually.
1 THESSALONIANS 5:17

THE PRAYER MAP®
FOR THE ENTIRE FAMILY. . .

The Prayer Map for Men
978-1-64352-438-2

The Prayer Map for Women
978-1-68322-557-7

The Prayer Map for Girls
978-1-68322-559-1

The Prayer Map for Boys
978-1-68322-558-4

The Prayer Map for Teens
978-1-68322-556-0

These purposeful prayer journals are a fun and creative way to more fully experience the power of prayer. Each page guides you to write out thoughts, ideas, and lists. . .which then creates a specific "map" for you to follow as you talk to God. Each map includes a spot to record the date, so you can look back on your prayers and see how God has worked in your life. *The Prayer Map* will not only encourage you to spend time talking with God about the things that matter most. . .it will also help you build a healthy spiritual habit of continual prayer for life!

Spiral Bound / $7.99